You Be the Judge

Sidney B. Carroll
YOU BE THE JUDGE
Illustrated by John Richmond

Lothrop, Lee and Shepard Co.,
NEW YORK

To Dean Joseph W. Hawley and Professor Graham Hughes
of the New York University Law School
and the children of the Whitby School–New Canaan ride
pool where the idea for this book was born

Contents

There was a time, before radio and television and movies, when people attended court sessions regularly, both for entertainment and to keep up with what was going on. A court was a familiar place where they could see real-life drama. They took sides and had strong opinions about the way each case was decided.

Because the people expressed their opinions freely, judges and others responsible for making the laws were constantly kept aware that the majority of the people have to believe that laws are just, or they won't respect and obey them.

Though we can still watch court sessions today, most of us are content to read about the outcome in the newspapers. We forget that as citizens it is up to us to make sure that our laws are just.

Justice is what we feel is the fairest thing to do once all the arguments are considered. If a problem has a simple solution, it is usually not necessary to bring it to court. Thus the cases that do come to court usually present difficult legal problems.

To make sure that the best possible justice is done, the legal system provides for appeals by losers (except for the government in a criminal case). Several appeals are usually allowed in order to ensure a thorough review of the issues. It is the decision of the highest court that settles the case which will be the law or precedent for the same kind of case from then on.

This is a book of legal problems and real legal cases for you to decide. The cases are appeals court decisions and all but one, the Palsgraf case, are still good law for deciding the same problem when it comes up again. But the decisions, like all legal decisions, may be changed in the next case like it if a fairer solution can be found.

Each actual legal case in this book is followed on the next page by the decision reached by the court. All the decisions are printed upside down, to give you a chance to make up your own mind about what you think is the fairest solution before you find out what the court decided.

How would *you* decide each of these cases?

You be the judge.

The Revolutionary and the Congressman

Try this problem which you might read about in a newspaper today.

Suppose a revolutionary wants some newspaper attention for his beliefs. He throws a lighted homemade bomb on the porch of the house of a Congressman who runs out the door and throws the bomb away. It hits the porch of the house next door and goes off, blowing pieces of wood into the street. One of them hurts a woman walking on the sidewalk. Who should pay for her injuries? The revolutionary? The Congressman?

If you were a lawyer for the injured woman you could argue in court with the help of the case on the next page which was decided in an English court in 1773. Our American law started from English law and includes many old English cases where they still contain the best solution to a problem. Law students call this The Gingerbread Man Case. It set a precedent which is still good law in a situation like this.

The Gingerbread Man Case

Shepard was feeling wild. It was a holiday and he was in the market watching a crowd of people buy food and play games in the open market hall. He took a firecracker out of his pocket, lighted it, and tossed it inside the building where it sizzled through the air and fell on a gingerbread stand owned by Yates. Willis, who was standing nearby, picked up the burning firecracker and threw it away. It landed on another gingerbread stand owned by Ryal who threw it out into the crowd where Scott was standing. The firecracker hit him in the eye and blew it out.

Could Scott make Willis, Ryal, or Shepard pay for his lost eye and his doctor bills?

Turn the book upside down for the judges' decision
in *The Gingerbread Man Case*

Shepard had to pay all of Scott's bills and a lot of money to him because Scott would have only one eye to see with for the rest of his life. One judge thought that because the firecracker had stopped moving when it fell on Yates's booth, the damage it did once it was thrown on was no longer Shepard's fault.

But the rest of the judges decided that because Shepard had started the whole thing he should be responsible for whatever happened, since both Willis and Ryal were only trying to get rid of a dangerous lighted firecracker in a hurry. This was the natural thing to do under the circumstances and not something for which they should be held responsible.

Scott v. Shepard
2 Wm. Bl. 892, 96 Eng. Rep. 525 (1773)

(These words and letters and numbers are the legal name of The Gingerbread Man Case. You will see all the cases in this book identified like this below the judges' decisions. If you would like to read the actual decision, you will be able to find it in any law library. The librarian will help you use the legal name to look up the case.)

The Inhospitable Householder

Suppose you are a lawyer and a young couple comes in to see you. The husband tells you that he and his pregnant wife were walking in a city street. Suddenly the sky turned very dark. People ran up the street yelling, "A tornado is coming!"

The husband says he pulled his wife onto the porch of a house where the owner was shutting the door because he was afraid of the tornado too. He wouldn't let the man and woman in. As the tornado rushed through the street, both of them were blown around and hurt.

Would you tell them they could win a suit in court against the houseowner?

See if you think the next case would help in your argument for the young couple if you decided to represent their suit.

The Case of the Sudden Storm

Ploof went for a sail on Lake Champlain with his wife and two children. Suddenly a bad storm blew up. Ploof headed for the nearest dock to tie up until it was over. He knew he was tying up at someone else's dock but did it anyway in order to save the family and the boat. Putnam, who owned the dock, wasn't at his cottage but his hired man, who was, went down to the dock and untied the boat. The boat was ruined in the storm. The people were saved but several of them suffered broken bones. In law the hired man acting for his boss is considered the same as his boss. Should Putnam have to pay for a new boat and for the Ploofs' doctor bills?

Usually Ploof would have no right to use Putnam's dock. That would be called trespassing and it is against the law. But there was an emergency in this situation; the storm came up quickly, without warning, making it impossible to go back to the Ploofs' dock. Since the boat and the lives of the people were in danger, Ploof and his family had a right to tie up to Putnam's dock until they could safely go out into the lake again. Under the circumstances, this was not trespassing. Putnam had to pay for the damage to the boat and to the people because he was responsible for what his hired man did while on the job.

Remember the young couple in the tornado. If you used *Ploof v. Putnam* as law to argue for them as their lawyer in court, what arguments could the houseowner make to defend himself?

Ploof v. Putnam
81 Vt. 471, 15 Ann.Cas. 1151 (1908)

The Palsgraf Case

A train has already started out of the station. As two railroad company guards try to help a man get on, they accidentally knock the small newspaper-covered package he is carrying to the tracks. There are fireworks in the package which go off, causing an explosion so strong that it tips over a set of scales on the platform many feet away. A woman standing nearby is struck by the falling scales and badly hurt.

Who should pay for her injuries?

1928

Mrs. Palsgraf, the woman who was hurt, sued the Long Island Railroad and lost (though she would probably win in a New York court with this case today). Her lawyer argued that since the railroad men had been careless when they knocked down the man's package, the railroad should be responsible for any harm which occurred as a direct result.

The railroad won, arguing that it was not the fault of its guards that Mrs. Palsgraf was hurt because they had not done anything to *her*. They could not have expected that she would be injured because of what they did to the package, since it didn't indicate that it had fireworks in it.

Palsgraf v. Long Island R.R. Co.
248 N.Y. 339, 162 N.E. 99 (1928)

The Kick in the Shins Case

Putney and Vosburg were eleven-year-old boys who sat across from each other in school. Putney gave Vosburg a kick in the shins. The kick was so small that Vosburg didn't feel it, but there was already a wound in his leg; the kick disturbed it and a serious infection developed. Doctor bills were high. Could Vosburg collect from Putney?

When the case was brought to court, the jury voted that Putney should pay Vosburg $2500. The case was appealed to a higher court. Should the appeals judge have upheld this decision?

Vosburg v. Putney
80 Wis. 523, 50 N.W. 403 (1891)

Putney lost his appeal. Even though he had no intention to hurt Vosburg badly, as shown by the fact that the kick was not even felt, Putney did intend the kick that touched the other boy. This is called a battery, an act that is against the law. The intent Putney had to kick Vosburg was enough to make him responsible for anything harmful resulting from the kick, even though there was already a wound in Vosburg's leg and without it there would not have been any infection at all.

1890

The Case of the Foul Ball

Hudson was sixty-five. He paid for a reserved seat at a baseball game and was hit by a foul ball and hurt. At the trial he told the court he thought the seat he was buying was protected by wire netting. It wasn't. Hudson argued that the Kansas City Baseball Club should pay his bills because it did not protect the grandstand where he sat or warn him of his lack of protection.

Should he have won his case?

Hudson lost. The judge pointed out that Hudson must have seen that he wasn't behind a net since there was no proof that his vision was poor. He had been to ball games before and knew, or should have known, that there was a chance a ball would come through and hit him. He chose to remain and should not expect to be paid. The principle on which this decision was made is called "assuming the risk," and simply means that when you know you may be hurt doing something but choose to do it anyway, it is your own fault if you do get hurt.

Hudson v. Kansas City Baseball Club
349 Mo. 1215, 164 S.W.2d 318 (1942)

1942

richmond

The Coronation Case

In England a king was to be crowned. Processions were planned which were going to march down the street past Henry's house. Krell rented the house for the coronation days so he and his friends could watch the ceremonies and parades. The prince became suddenly so sick that the coronation was canceled two days before it was supposed to take place. Could Krell have his money back?

Krell could have his money back. The people making the agreement or contract understood that the rooms were rented for a particular purpose and no other. Krell and Henry assumed there would be a coronation ceremony. Since it did not take place, the contract was considered without meaning and could not be enforced.

Krell v. Henry (1903)
L.R. 2 K.B. 740

RENTAL
AGREEMENT

1903

richmond

The Case of
the Collapsing Building

Mr. Stees owns some land. He makes a written contract with Mr. Leonard, a builder, to put up a business building on the land according to a plan which they agree on. The masons and carpenters begin to work. They build the building three stories high. Then it falls to the ground. The next year, the builders try again. When the building has reached three stories it again falls to the ground because the soil underneath is quicksand and cannot hold a building whenever a lot of water is in the ground.

Should Mr. Leonard have to pay Mr. Stees for the money he didn't make in his business because the building wasn't finished?

The judge said that Leonard could have written it into the contract that he would not put up the building if unknown problems in the land made it impossible to build on it with- out draining it first. Since Leonard had agreed to build without any qualifications in the contract, he owed Stees for what he had lost in business because the building did not go up.

Stees v. Leonard

20 Minn. (Gilfillan Edition) 448, (1874)

30

1874

The Kentucky Derby Case

McDevitt was a jockey. He had a contract with the owner to ride a horse named Grace in the Kentucky Derby. Stokes was not the owner but wanted Grace to win because he owned some of her horse relatives who would be worth more if she won. He promised McDevitt he would give him a thousand dollars if he won the Kentucky Derby on Grace. McDevitt and Grace did win, but Stokes refused to pay the money he had promised. Could McDevitt get the court to force him to pay?

McDevitt could not collect the thousand dollars. Under his contract with the owner he already had a duty to ride the horse and try to win the race. Therefore he had promised nothing extra to Stokes for the thousand dollars and there was no contract with him. For a contract to exist, each side must promise to give something to the other which he does not already have to do for someone else.

Today most states have laws which say that if a man writes and signs a promise to pay money, the court can force him to pay even though the man who is to receive the money doesn't have to do anything for it.

McDevitt v. Stokes
174 Ky. 515, 192 S.W. 681 (1917)

Grandma and Goldilocks

Grandma said to her granddaughter Goldilocks, "Here is a ring which I will give to you. Try it on."

Goldilocks tried it on and told her grandmother that it was too small. Grandma said:

"It will need to be made bigger. Let me take it and wear it until I am through with it. But the ring is yours."

A few days later, Grandma died. Goldilocks claimed the ring, but Grandma's heirs refused to give it to her. Is the ring legally hers?

1888

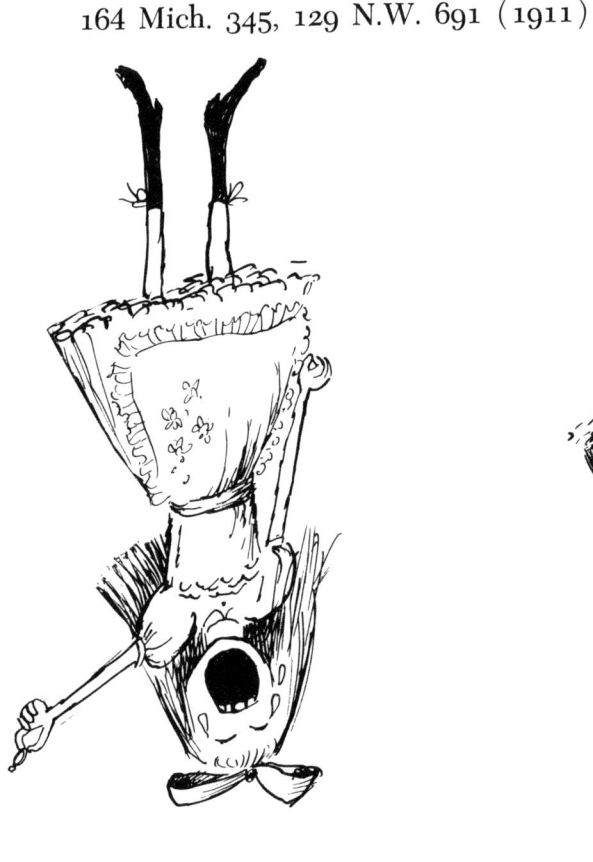

The court decided that Goldilocks could not have the ring. Grandma's words showed that she intended Goldilocks to have it sometime but not then. Even though she gave it to her granddaughter, it was only in her hand a minute or two, which was not enough to force a court to recognize it as a gift. Under the law it is necessary to show that a gift is given with the intention that it is to be owned by the other person *at that moment* and from then on. Also the person who receives it must keep it in such a way as to show that it is permanently his.

Facts transposed from:
Garrison v. Union Trust Co.
164 Mich. 345, 129 N.W. 691 (1911)

The Bungalow Case

Several families rented some land and built summer cabins there on top of cinder blocks. The blocks were not sunk into the ground, but there were water and electrical connections. Then the land was sold by the owner. Who owned the cabins?

The judge said that the cabins were houses but they were not permanent. This was lucky for the people who put them there because it meant they could have them and take them away. If the judge had called them permanent they would have been classified as fixtures and therefore would have belonged to the landowner even though the renting families had paid for putting them in. A cabin with a dug-in foundation would probably have been called permanent and would have had to be left there.

Sigrol Realty Corp. v. Valcich
12 A.D. 2d 430 (1961) aff'd 11 N. Y. 2d 668 (1962)

The Treasure Trove Case

A church in Wisconsin had a Carpet Rag Committee which collected rags from many places and gave them out to women who were paid to weave them into rugs for sale to benefit the church. Mrs. Zech received a bundle of rags and started to work.

She found twenty-one hundred dollars hidden in the center of one ball of rags. After advertising this in two newspapers, she gave the money to the Carpet Rag Committee to keep safe in case the owner turned up. When no one appeared to claim it after a long period of time, Mrs. Zech asked for the money back. The Committee refused to give it to her. Could she win a suit for it in court?

Zech v. Accola
253 Wis. 80, 33 N.W. 2d 232 (1948)

The Carpet Rag Committee claimed that Mrs. Zech had not done enough according to a Wisconsin statutory law to find the true owner. Though she had not done all the law required, Mrs. Zech had advertised the finding of the money in two newspapers. The court decided that this was a reasonable effort and sufficient to allow Mrs. Zech to keep the money, which was what the law calls "treasure trove." That is, it went unnoticed by the Carpet Rag Committee while it owned the rags so it never owned the money, and as far as Mrs. Zech was concerned it was the same as though she had found it in the street.

1948

TWO CRIMINAL CASES

Criminal prosecutions require a different kind of intent from that required in civil suits.

I n the problem about the revolutionary and the Congressman, the woman who was hurt had a right to sue the revolutionary who threw the bomb. She would do so as a private person bringing a civil suit.

The government would also prosecute the bomb thrower, in a separate criminal case. When an action is considered to be a danger to society, the government acts for all of us by prosecuting the person responsible.

In a civil case all that is required is that the one being sued intended to do or carelessly did an act which did harm. Since a criminal case hurts a person's reputation and may put him in jail, the defendant must have intended to do the exact harm he is charged with if he is to be convicted.

The Case of
the Borrowed Bicycle

A seventeen-year-old boy named Brown was working for his board at a house where the boy in the family kept throwing oranges at him. Brown didn't like this so he decided to take the boy's bike and hide it for a day. Actually, he made a mistake and took another boy's bike. He hid it under some brush in a hole, planning to return it in the evening, but he was caught before he could do so. Could Brown be convicted of a crime?

1894

richmond

Brown could not be convicted of stealing the bike. This would be the crime called larceny. To be guilty Brown would have had to intend not only to take the bike but also to keep the owner from ever getting it back.

If Brown had broken the bicycle after he took it, the owner could have won a civil case demanding payment for the damage. Intending to take the bike and using it would have been enough wrong for Brown to be required to pay for the harm done.

People v. Brown
105 Cal. 66, 38 Pac. 518 (1894)

The Accidental Murder

Thorne went into a store with a loaded gun, intending to rob it. He pointed the gun at the owner and told him to hold up his hands. The gun went off accidentally, killing the man. Then Thorne emptied the cash register and fled.

Could the state convict Thorne for murder?

Remember that in a criminal case, the accused must intend to do the very act he is accused of.

Thorne was convicted of murder. Though he had intended only to rob his victim, not to kill him, he was convicted for a special kind of murder called felony murder. Thorne's intention to commit the serious crime (or felony) of robbery is considered enough intent on his part to commit murder if it turns out that he kills someone in the course of the robbery.

State v. Thorne
39 Utah 208, 117 Pac. 58 (1911)

There are no more cases in this book. But you don't have to stop thinking about the law or learning more about it. If you know any judges or lawyers, talk with them. They'll remember the cases you've solved and will enjoy discussing them with you. You could go to the court nearest you and watch cases being tried.

There will always be problems to analyze and solve in daily life. Though these problems are not brought to court, they are still "cases" which you can have fun deciding just as you did the ones here. And when you do this you will be doing important work.

Decisions like the ones you have read here are called "common law" because their power comes not from the legislature but directly from the people themselves, and the people base their approval and willingness to obey on their own experience and beliefs. A judge won't change the law on the basis of a new argument unless he believes that the majority of the people will believe he is right. This means that in the long run the law is as just as is the people's thinking about right and wrong—the kind of thinking which you have done with this book and which each of us has many chances to do every day.

48

2   3   4   5   75   74   73   72